To

_____

From

_____

Date

_____

Little Prayers
for
Little Kids

Stormie Omartian
Artwork by Shari Warren

HARVEST HOUSE PUBLISHERS
EUGENE, OREGON

This book is dedicated to all the little children whom Jesus loves so dearly, and to those who teach them to pray.

It's never too early to teach a child to pray. This collection of short, memorable prayers is designed to help children learn to thank God for all He has given them, to ask for help in learning, to recognize His love for them, and to express their love for Him.

—Stormie Omartian

Good Morning, Jesus, I'm Awake

Good morning, Jesus, I'm awake.
Thank You for this brand-new day.
I'm happy that You always hear me
When I talk to You and pray.

Thank You, God, for the Color BLUE

Thank You, God, for the color **BLUE**,
The color of the sky and the ocean too.
Thank You for the color **GREEN**,
The color of the trees I've seen.

And for **RED**—like the car at the end of a train
And the colors in a rainbow after a rain.
Thank You that my eyes can see
All the colors You've made for me.

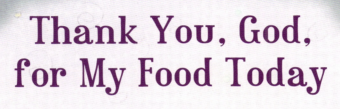

Thank You, God, for My Food Today

Thank You, God, for my food today

And caring for me in every way.

Help me learn to love it all—

The food that makes me strong and tall.

Thank You, God, That I Can Hear

Thank You, God, that I can hear

The dog that barks, the bird that sings,

And the telephone when it rings.

The splash of rain against the street,

People laughing when they meet.

Lord, I Want to Read like the Bigger Kids Do

Lord, I want to read like the bigger kids do.

Help me learn to do it easily.

Thank You for the many books

My friends and family read to me.

Thank You, Jesus, That You Love Me

Thank You, Jesus, that You love me.
I want to say, "I love You too!"
Thank You for watching over me
Wherever I go and whatever I do.

Jesus, Help Me to Obey

Jesus, help me to obey

What my mommy and daddy say.

Help me pick up my toys

And put them away

At the end of every day.

Lord, Help Me Learn to Set the Table

Lord, help me learn to set the table,

And bake some cookies when I'm able,

And clear my plate when dinner is through,

And help my family like You want me to.

Thank You, God, for the Gentle Rain

Thank You, God, for the gentle rain

That splashes on the windowpane.

When Mom says it's safe to go out for a while,

I jump and splash, and that makes me smile.

God, Teach Me to Love My Family and Friends

God, teach me to love my family and friends

The way that You love me.

You have love that never ends,

And that's the way I want to be.

Jesus, Help Me to Get Well

Jesus, help me to get well
Whenever I feel ill.
And comfort me when I am hurt.
Thank You that You always will.

Thank You, Dear God, for the Animals

Thank You, dear God, for the animals

Like little lambs and cats and dogs,

Big elephants, giraffes, bears, and frogs,

Horses, lions, zebras, and birds,

Goats and cows that travel in herds.

Seeing them is so much fun.

Thank You that You made each one.

Thank You, Lord, for the Water I Drink

Thank You, Lord, for the water I drink,

And for washing my hands at the sink,

And for my bath after I play,

The perfect end to a happy day.

Thank You, God, for My Cozy Bed

Thank You, God, for my cozy bed

And the pillow for my head.

Thank You for my blanket too,

So I can rest when day is through.

I'll sleep until the morning light,

But now it's time to say good night.

Good Night, Jesus, I'm Going to Sleep

Good night, Jesus, I'm going to sleep,
And I'm giving You my heart to keep.
Make my dreams the happy kind
So I wake up smiling in my mind.